D1709704

BEARING WITNESS
GENOCIDE AND ETHNIC CLEANSING IN THE MODERN WORLD™

CANADA'S
FIRST NATIONS AND
CULTURAL GENOCIDE

ROBERT Z. COHEN

ROSEN
PUBLISHING

NEW YORK

Published in 2017 by The Rosen Publishing Group, Inc.
29 East 21st Street, New York, NY 10010

Library of Congress Cataloging-in-Publication Data

Names: Cohen, Robert Z., author.
Title: Canada's First Nations and Cultural Genocide / Robert Z. Cohen.
Description: New York : Rosen Publishing, 2017. | Series: Bearing Witness: Genocide and Ethnic Cleansing in the Modern World | Includes bibliographical references and index.
Identifiers: LCCN 2015050843 | ISBN 9781508171621 (library bound)
Subjects: LCSH: Indians of North America—Canada—Social conditions. | Indians of North America—Canada—Cultural assimilation. | Indians of North America—Education—Canada. | Off-reservation boarding schools—Canada.
Classification: LCC E78.C2 C597 2016 | DDC 971.004/97—dc23
LC record available at http://lccn.loc.gov/2015050843

Manufactured in China

CONTENTS

INTRODUCTION

Canada is one of the most successfully diverse nations in the world today. The English and French languages share official status. Immigrant cultures enrich its cities. The culture of its Native peoples—First Nations, Inuit, and Métis—is vibrant and alive. But those Native peoples suffered for more than a century. Their system of school education was designed to remove Native children from their homes, destroy their culture, and forbid their languages. It also forced them to melt into the fabric of Canadian life. Indian identity and birthright came under strong attack. Generations of aboriginal children were abused and traumatized. All this thanks to the official effort to absorb them into a nation that did not want "Indians." Today, Native Canadians have again found their voice. They are speaking out about the experience of the residential school system. They are questioning the official policy that robbed so many of them of their heritage. Native children lost their Native identity. Their Native languages were silenced. They were forcibly removed from their homes and abused. This has come to be seen as a shameful history of "cultural genocide."

The Dominion of Canada established itself as an independent federation in 1867. And the first inhabitants of the land, the First Nations, were seen as a "problem." The solution offered by the Canadian system was assimilation. However, this meant that Native people would have to lose their own unique

Survivors of a school system that tried to make Indian identity disappear, Native people play a strong role in Canadian culture today.

culture and identity. According to John S. Milloy in his book *A National Crime*, in 1920 the deputy superintendent of Canada's Department of Indian Affairs, poet Duncan Campbell Scott, wrote, "I want to get rid of the Indian problem…Our objective is to continue until there is not a single Indian in Canada that has not been absorbed into the body politic and there is no Indian question, and no Indian Department."

Today, Canadians look back on this cruel history with shame. They struggle to come to terms with the generations of trauma inflicted on Native children in the name of "civilization." Canadians have established a Truth and Reconciliation Commission to help make sense of a cruel and harmful past. Both Native and immigrant Canadians are involved. Native Canadians are a significant group. They make up almost 5 percent of Canada's population, with larger concentrations in the western provinces and in the territory of Nunavut. (Less than 1 percent of the United States claims Native American descent.) "Indians" can no longer be ignored. Native Canadians have begun to reclaim their culture and languages. They are actively working on a global scale to help indigenous people around the world assert their legal rights and reverse the damage of cultural genocide.

CHAPTER 1

FROM KANATA TO CANADA

The indigenous people of Canada—the First Nations, Inuit, and Métis people who were known for hundreds of years as "Indians"—have a long history of contact with Europeans. Five hundred years ago, the French and the British arrived with the intention of possessing the new lands that they had discovered. The kings of France and England saw the New World as a source of land and wealth for their kingdoms. Europeans were sent as settlers to make the New World into an overseas version of the countries they had left behind. The first inhabitants—the First Nations—had developed many cultures with a much different understanding about the land they lived on. They would not allow their land and traditions to be taken from them easily.

The first meetings of the First Nations peoples along the St. Lawrence River and the Europeans were based on trading furs for European products. The French and British had settled along the coastal arcas, but beyond lay the frontier, a land that was far beyond the control of European powers. The French explorer Jacques Cartier was the first to establish a European

Jacques Cartier's discovery of the St. Lawrence River, depicted here by painter Théodore Gudin, opened up the vast lands of Canada to Europeans eager to harvest beaver fur.

presence in the new land. Sailing into the broad St. Lawrence River, Cartier landed at the Iroquois town of Stadacona, near modern Quebec City, in 1534 and claimed the land for the king of France. He called it "New France" while the local Iroquois people called it "Kanata"—meaning "town." The French in Canada settled safely near their forts in Quebec and Montreal. Fur traders called *voyageurs* paddled huge canoes through the network of rivers and lakes to trade with Native communities for the luxurious beaver furs that were valued in Europe. In return, Native people received guns with which to kill more beavers, and acquire more guns.

CULTURAL GENOCIDE

The word "genocide" first came into use during World War II to describe the Nazi mass murder of Jewish people in the Holocaust. It has since come to be applied to any destruction with the intent to destroy a racial, religious, ethnic, or national group. Cases of genocide have occurred throughout history: against Armenians, in Cambodia, against Native American communities in North and South America, and more recently in Rwanda, the Sudan, and the former Yugoslavia.

Genocide was recognized as a crime by the United Nations soon after World War II. Article 2 of the 1948 United Nations Convention on the Prevention and Punishment of the Crime of Genocide lays out the definition: "Any of the following acts committed with intent to destroy, in whole or in part, a national, ethnical, racial or religious group, as such: killing members of the group; causing serious bodily or mental harm to members of the group; deliberately inflicting on the group conditions of life, calculated to bring about its physical destruction in whole or in part; imposing measures intended to prevent births within the group; [and] forcibly transferring children of the group to another group."

The removal of children to be brought up by another group is a way to force them to lose their culture and identity. Cultural genocide happens when a government or state tries to destroy a people's special identity by forbidding their language, religion, way of life, or ability to live together according to their traditional culture, although

Continued on next page

Continued from previous page

the law has never settled the definition of "cultural geno-cide." The destruction of many of the Native cultures in both North and South America are cases of cultural geno-cide. Cultural genocide can include Chinese government attempts to erase indigenous Tibetan language and culture. In 1971, Cree First Nations writer Harold Cardinal used the term "cultural genocide" to describe how the Canadian residential school system erased Native cultural identity by physically removing children from their families for years, cutting them off from their language and culture.

THE BEAVER WARS

In 1608, the French traders and their First Nations allies attacked the rival Iroquois confederacy in New York. This started a century of conflict, which has come to be known as the Beaver Wars. It is perhaps the most destructive war in North American history, from both war and disease. The Iroquois received guns from the Dutch and English. When Native communities traded furs for guns, they were exposed to new European diseases for which they had no natural immunity, such as measles or chicken pox. Diseases soon spread to communities that had not yet even met a European trader. Entire nations of people were devastated. It is estimated that as much as 90 percent of North America's indigenous population may have died of Old World diseases introduced between 1500 and 1750.

FIRST PEOPLE, FIRST NATIONS

When Christopher Columbus arrived in the New World in 1492, he believed he had discovered a new route to India and called the people he met "Indians." The name stuck. To this day Native people themselves often use it, especially in the United States, although the term "Native American" has gradually come into favor. In Canada, however, the term "aboriginal" refers to all those who are descended from the first inhabitants of the land, including Inuit and Métis. "Native" and "indigenous" are still commonly used to refer to people originating in a particular place. "Indian" has come to represent the legal definition of a person with "Indian status" based on treaty rights. "First Nations" has gradually come to replace the term "Indian." Canadians don't use the word "tribe" to refer to Native communities. A First Nation may refer to a particular group or reserve, as in Shubenacadie First Nation in Nova Scotia or Kainai Nation in Alberta. "Inuit" refers to the people of the Arctic—once known by the word "Eskimo"—who are indigenous and native to Canada but not legally considered First Nations. "Métis" is the term for people who were born to a mixed heritage of Native and European blood. They are Native but not classified as "status Indians."

The Hudson Bay Company preferred to hire local Native people to work as trappers and boatmen for their great trading empire.

TOP HATS AND CROWNS: THE FUR TRADE

French Canada came under the rule of the British crown following the conquest of Quebec City in 1760 during the French and Indian War (also known in Canada as the Seven Years' War, and in French Canada as the War of Conquest). When the United States declared its independence from the king of England in 1776, Canada remained a loyal outpost of the British crown and became a safe haven for loyalist American refugees. The British crown depended on peaceful trade and military relationships with neighboring First Nations such as the Mohawk, Odawa, and Anishnaabe of the Great Lakes. When the United States invaded Canada during the War of 1812, the Shawnee leader Tecumseh led a united force of First Nations people under British command against the American invaders.

During the nineteenth century, Canada avoided the vicious wars against the Indians that became a constant feature of the American frontier. There were far fewer Euro-Canadians to settle the vast forests and plains, and Native peoples were the key to obtaining the most valuable natural resource: furs. In Europe, top hats had come into fashion, and beaver fur provided the best felt for making hats. In 1670, King Charles II awarded contracts to the Hudson's Bay Company to control the fur trade. By 1860, the Hudson's Bay Company grew to control most of western Canada. That was nearly 15 percent of the world's surface! The company set up a network of trading forts. Most of the trappers were First Nations people or the descendants of the French voyageurs intermarried with local First Nations women, creating a unique society mixing Native and French traditions called Métis. The Métis trapped, traded, and roamed the plains where they hunted the vast herds of buffalo to make pemmican, which was dried buffalo meat mixed with fat and berries. It was used as a survival food by Hudson's Bay Company trappers.

The world was changing rapidly, and First Nations people were aware of the advantages to be had by adopting the white man's education. Christian missionaries had long worked among Native communities in an effort to convert them to the Christian religion. In 1840, a Methodist missionary in Manitoba named James

Trappers had little time to hunt for food and depended instead on pemmican, a high-calorie dried meat that did not go bad over time.

Evans developed a special alphabet for the Cree language. It was easy to learn and adapted well to the Inuit language, and it remains in use to this day. Early Native education was in the hands of Catholic and Protestant missionaries working to convert Natives away from their indigenous beliefs.

SHINGWAUK'S TEACHING WIGWAM

In 1832, an Anishnaabe chief named Shingwauk traveled on snowshoe from Sault Ste. Marie on the Great Lakes to Toronto to ask the governor of Upper Canada for help starting a school for Native children. According to J. R. Miller's book, Shingwauk said, "I hoped before I die I should see a big teaching wigwam built at Garden River where children from the Great Chippeway Lake would be received and clothed and fed and taught how to read and write, and also how to farm and build houses, and also how to make clothing, so that by-and-bye they might go back and teach their own people." Shingwauk's dream was to help children learn modern skills but not abandon their own language, culture, and traditional beliefs. Soon a school was built, and by 1875 it was expanded into the first Indian residential school ready to educate and house Native children from far away. For many children, however, Shingwauk's dream would become a nightmare.

CHAPTER 2

"BRING THEM TO CIVILIZATION"

Canada is unique among Britain's former colonies. It developed a system to unite the former colonies through patient negotiation and cooperation with the British crown without violence. Britain's four colonies in Canada were horrified by the American Civil War. And after the 1867 purchase of Alaska from Russia, it feared the United States would expand its territorial claims. On July 1, 1867, the four British colonies of Canada declared themselves a federation as the Dominion of Canada, remaining a loyal member of the British Commonwealth with the British monarch at its helm. English- and French-speaking Canadians carefully defined their legal rights. Only the First Nations were left out. The new government did not want First Nations people to continue to act as independent groups or nations. Beginning in 1871, a series of eleven treaties was signed with First Nations in the western regions of Canada. They set aside reserve lands for First Nations. The treaties allowed the Dominion of Canada to open lands for new immigrants to move to the West to farm, but it also made First Nations wards of the state. Power was now held in the office of a government-appointed superintendent, and not by the traditional First Nations chiefs.

The Canada Pacific Railroad was completed in 1885, opening the West to immigrant settlement and industrial growth. The great buffalo herds were gone, and the market for furs had collapsed. The First Nations were seen as a stumbling block in the march toward "civilization." The plan of the government was to assimilate Native people, to "bring them to civilization" so that they would not claim legal rights as separate and unique communities. To do this the government had to destroy Native identity, and the easiest way to do that was to use schools to remove children from the influence of their parents and communities.

THE INDIAN ACT OF 1876

In 1876, the Canadian Parliament passed the Indian Act. Until that time, First Nations had made treaty agreements with the crown of Britain and not with individual Canadian provinces. The Indian Act guaranteed that the federal government of Canada would be in a powerful position

Like many European-born Canadians in the nineteenth century, Prime Minister John A. Macdonald showed little respect for aboriginal rights.

to control the First Nations. The Indian Act defined who was an Indian and set aside rules for reserves, like reservations, for First Nations communities, which were defined as "bands." The law was designed to increase assimilation pressures on First Nations. Looking back on the Indian Act, according to John Milloy, Canada's first prime minister, John A. Macdonald, said in 1887, "The great aim of our legislation has been to do away with the tribal system and assimilate the Indian people in all respects with the other inhabitants of the Dominion as speedily as they are fit to change." The Indian Act promoted enfranchisement, which would force aboriginal people to accept life as citizens and not as "status Indians" of a First Nations community. If a First Nations person acquired a university education, that person would lose Indian status. If a First Nations woman married a non-Indian man, she would lose her legal status as an Indian.

Later additions to the Indian Act further restricted aboriginal freedoms. Important First Nations traditional religious rituals such as the Potlatch ceremony on the Pacific coast and the Sun Dance on the prairies were banned and made illegal in 1885. In 1911, the Indian Act allowed the government to take Native land for roads and public building projects. In 1914, a law decreed that First Nations were not allowed to wear traditional clothing and regalia without permission. In 1927, a new provision made it impossible for First Nations to hire a lawyer to make legal claims against Canada.

The Indian Act is still in effect, although it has been changed many times. First Nations people often express concern that without the Indian Act the Canadian government would not recognize those special rights that come with their Indian status.

The Indian Act came at a bad time for many aboriginal communities. Now confined to reserves, and with no tradition or experience with farming, many First Nations found themselves starving. They turned to the government for the food help it had promised in the treaties, but it did not arrive. To force First Nations off the open prairies and onto reserves, Prime Minister John A. Macdonald had declared in 1880 that his government would be "rigid, even stingy" in distributing food to starving First Nations "until the Indians are on the verge of starvation, to reduce the expense." If the First Nations wanted their children to avoid starvation, they were told to send their children away to residential schools where they would be fed and educated in the white man's ways.

MÉTIS PEOPLE

The Indian Act also stripped the Métis people of their Indian status. The Métis are the mixed blood descendants of French Canadian and Scottish fur traders and Native women found in communities all across Canada. The word "Métis" means "mixed" in French. Most spoke French and Cree. Even today many Métis speak a unique language called Michif, which mixes Native Cree verbs and grammar with French nouns. Métis enjoyed good relations with First Nations communities, hunting, trading, and intermarrying with them. The Métis living along the Red River in Manitoba, near today's Winnipeg, had traded with the Hudson's Bay Company for a long time. When Canada purchased the Red River Country from the Hudson's Bay Company in 1869, the Métis faced losing title to their land. Louis Riel led a revolt against the government of Canada. The revolt was quickly put down, and Riel was exiled to the United States. Riel returned in 1885 and again raised an armed force of Métis and allied Cree. After a few initial victories, the Canadian army at the Battle of Batoche defeated the Métis and Cree in 1885. Louis Riel was tried and hanged for treason. Métis were not recognized as having Indian status and could not attend Indian schools. They were also unwelcome in white schools. Many Métis parents actually paid to have their children attend Indian residential school. For many years Métis people faced racism and discrimination, both as minority French speakers and as mixed-blood people. Today they are recognized in Canada as an aboriginal people with rights similar to that of First Nations and Inuit.

THE DAVIN REPORT

The Canadian government was shocked by the violence of the Riel Rebellion. Canada had previously avoided frontier violence. More than ever before, the government in Ottawa felt the need to assimilate First Nations people and make them accept

After his first rebellion was lost, Métis leader Louis Riel spent years as a refugee in the United States. Métis people remember him as a hero.

Residential school students studied in the morning but spent hours doing unpaid farm labor or toiling in workshops until the evening.

and adopt the European culture. The key to the goal of assimilation was the aboriginal child. Until the 1870s, if Native children were educated, it was at local reserve day schools. Christian churches ran them. In 1879, Prime Minister Macdonald sent the writer Nicholas Davin to the United States to report on the large, centralized Indian schools that had been set up in Carlisle, Pennsylvania, and Hampton, Virginia. These schools removed Indian children from their families and reservations to teach them skills like farming and factory work. Davin was convinced that such large-scale "industrial schools" would be better suited to Canada's purposes. In Milloy's book, Davin's report stated, "The chief thing to do when dealing with less civilized or wholly barbarous tribes was to separate the children from the parents." Davin was impressed with the director of the Carlisle Indian School, former U.S. military man Richard Henry Pratt, who felt that to achieve success one had to "Kill the Indian to save the man," according to the Smithsonian.

Former prime minister John Macdonald, serving as superintendent general of Indian Affairs, fully agreed with the Davin Report, telling the Canadian House of Commons in

1883, "When the school is on the reserve, the child lives with its parents, who are savages, and though he may learn to read and write, his habits and training mode of thought are Indian. He is simply a savage who can read and write…Indian children should be withdrawn as much as possible from the parental influence, and the only way to do that would be to put them in central training industrial schools where they will acquire the habits and modes of thought of white men."

The Davin Report led to the building of large "residential" schools, each designed to house hundreds of Native children. The goal was to teach the children English and farming skills, with the hope that on leaving school they would settle on individual farms and not return to the shared community of First Nations traditional life. Christian churches would be active partners in operating the schools, cutting costs by using missionaries as teachers. By 1930, there were already eighty such residential schools across Canada.

The government estimate of the amount of money to feed all the children at the schools was far short of what was needed. Schools had to turn to churches for extra money, which allowed church missionary projects to take control of the staff and teachers of the schools. Dishonest school administrators often stole money that was to be spent on food and clothing for students. The teachers were paid low wages and were often not qualified to teach in a regular school. When the Methodist church at Mount Elgin School suggested training aboriginal people to be teachers, wrote Milloy, the idea was met with racism: "the experience with Indian teachers has not been happy."

CHAPTER 3

STOLEN CHILDREN, STOLEN LANGUAGES

The European view of Native children was that they were savages who lacked culture and civilization. In reality they were raised among their families in complex societies that were perfectly adapted to the resources of the land—whether in the deep forest, the frozen Arctic, or the rocky Pacific coast. Native languages had developed words that fully described all the things a person would need to live on the land, such as plants, animals, people, and the relationships between them. A Native child's education came from observing his or her family in the bush. Mabel Brown was a survivor of the schools from the Northwest Territories. She remembered to the Truth and Reconciliation Commission of Canada's (TRC) report *The Survivors Speak*, "You know life in the bush is really good. And when we were growing up we went, when my dad was alive, him and my mom brought us out into the bush. And we went as a family together… they taught us how to do things. They'd tell us first, they'd show us, and then we'd do it and then that's how we learned that." Taking children away from their families was the first step in taking them from their language and culture, and from the ability for them to live on the land as their ancestors had for thousands of years.

In 1884, a new amendment to the Indian Act required Native children to attend government-run schools. Later, an amendment to the Indian Act in 1920 stated that all Native children had to attend an Indian school. It also made it illegal for them to attend any other school.

"WHY DID YOU LET US GO?"

Local Indian superintendents tracked down children in remote Native communities and would threaten parents with jail unless they surrendered their children. In 2008, the Truth and Reconciliation Commission began to collect the childhood stories of elder survivors of the residential school system. Linda Pahpasay Mcdonald from Ontario told the TRC,

> I looked outside, my mom was, you know, crying, and I see my dad grabbing her, and, I was wondering why, why my mom was struggling. She told me many years later what happened, and she explained to me why we had to be sent away to, to residential school...and I used to ask her, "Why did you let us go, like, why didn't you stop them? Why didn't you come and get us?" And she told me, "We couldn't, because they told us if we tried to do anything, like, get you guys back, we'd be thrown into jail."

Some parents hoped their children would use the experience of residential schooling for the benefit of their people. Shirley Williams told the TRC that when was sent to the Spanish, Ontario, girls' school, her father gave her four instructions: "One was remember who you are. Do not forget your language. Whatever they do to you in there, be strong. And the fourth one, learn about the Indian Act, and come back and teach me… you don't know why I'm telling you this, but some day you will understand.'"

Most Native children had never left their home and parents. Then the Indian agents arrived to take them away to school, wrote Larry Loyie, which was often hundreds of miles away from home. "My two sisters and I were picked up by dog sled," said Lina Schott Gallup of the Cree/Dene First Nations to the TRC. "The Northwest Mounted police took us from Fort MacKay to Fort Murray. Before we took another train to Grouard the nuns put us in a tub filled with hot water. We thought they were going to cook us! Our trip to school was 847 kilometers [526 miles]. We never went back home. We lost our language because we weren't allowed to speak it."

ARRIVAL AT SCHOOL

Arriving at school was confusing and often uncomfortable for Native children. Many had never been to a town or city, ridden on a railroad, or seen a large school building. Talking to the TRC, Calvin Myerion remembered the school in Brandon, Alberta: "The only building I knew at that time was the one

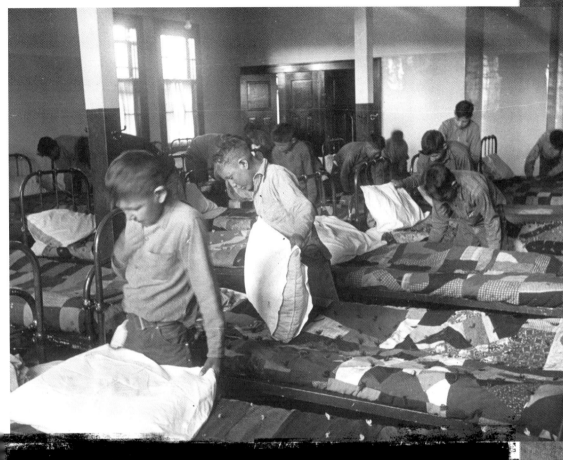

Most children had never left their families and communities before being sent away to schools. The loneliness caused many to run away.

story house we had…and when I got to the residential school I seen [*sic*] this big monster of a building, and I'd never seen any buildings that large, that high…I've always called it a monster, still do today, not because of the size of it, but because of the things that happened there."

25

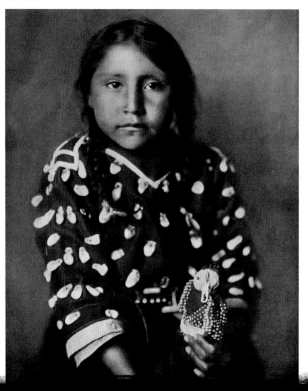

Cutting children's hair and forbidding their clothing was a way to make students ashamed of their Native identity.

As soon as the children arrived, they were made to feel ashamed of their appearance and Native identity. They were given baths and forced to hand over their clothing. Anything they had brought from home was replaced by school clothing, which was often used and repaired. Then their hair was cut. For aboriginal people hair often has significant meaning. Helen Harry told the TRC about her first day at the school in Williams Lake, British Columbia: "I remember really not wanting to cut my hair, because I remember my mom had really long hair down to her waist. And she never, ever cut it, and she didn't cut our hair either…and I kept saying that I didn't want to cut my hair but they just sat me on the chair and they just got scissors and they just grabbed my hair and they just cut it. And they had this big bucket there, and they just threw everybody's hair in the bucket…" When Charlie Bigknife's hair was cut off at the File Hills School he was told, "Now you are no longer an Indian," he explained in the Truth and Reconciliation Commission of Canada's report *They Came for the Children*.

The next step in admitting the children to their new lives at school was to assign each of them a number, which identified their clothes and shoes, which bed was theirs, and which work was to be assigned to each of them. Wilbur Abrahams remembered to the TRC, "They told us to remember our numbers. Instead of calling our name, they would call my number, and if you don't remember your number, you get yelled at…You had to keep memorizing your number. Mine was 989."

A RICH TRADITION OF LANGUAGE

Most children arriving at the residential schools spoke the aboriginal languages they had learned from their families and used in the Native communities. These languages were, perhaps, the strongest bond that defined Native communities. Traditional knowledge was taught in Native languages, and each community kept alive their values and history through stories and ceremonies expressed in their local tongue. North America had more than three hundred

Continued on next page

Continued from previous page

different languages. Some were small and local, while some, like Cree and the Dene languages, were spread over thousands of miles. Some of the languages are as different from each other as English is from Chinese. Some belong to a related family of languages, just like French, Spanish, and Italian belong to the Romance language family. The Algonquin family of related languages is very widespread, including Cree, Odawa, Innu, and Ojibwa (also known as Anishnaabe), as well as Blackfoot and Mi'kmaq. Many Native people spoke several languages, while some "mixed" languages, such as Michif, Bungee, and Chinook Jargon, developed through contact with white traders.

In many Native homes today, the traditional language is not being taught to children. The experience of the residential schools caused many Native children to stop using or forget their languages. Today, most Native communities in North America have to rely on English or French to communicate. Native languages are disappearing from aboriginal communities, although children are still learning Cree, Ojibwa, Inuktitut, and Mi'kmaq. In many communities efforts are being made to revive Native languages and teach them to children before the last elderly speakers pass on.

FORBIDDEN TONGUES

The Department of Indian Affairs decided that use of English in the schools was the only sure way to assimilate Native children. The department report of 1886 stated, "English or French

Acclaimed actress Tamara Podemski studied the Ojibwa language in order to reclaim her identity as an Anishnaabe person. Almost all Native languages are in danger of disappearing.

should be the only means of communication," wrote Milloy. When children arrived at the residential schools they were immediately forbidden to speak in their Native languages. Often, rewards or punishments were used to force children to abandon their home languages. At Shingwauk School, children who did not speak their languages might win a bag of nuts as a reward.

Punishment was waiting for children who could not speak English. William Antoine grew up speaking Ojibwa and was sent to the school in Spanish, Ontario. He told the TRC, "I was in grade one and the work that was given to me, I didn't know anything about and the teacher was speaking English to me and I didn't understand what he was saying…and he would get mad at me and angry…I couldn't do it because I didn't understand what he was saying. It was so hard." Beatings were common punishments. Alan Kavik was beaten with a leather strap for speaking his Native Inuit language. He explained to the TRC, "I couldn't speak English, they tell me to speak English but I couldn't help it, I had to speak my Inuktitut language. When I speak my Inuktitut language they, the teachers, strapped, strapped, strapped me, pulled my ears, made me stand in a corner all morning."

Removed from their Native language communities for many of their most important growing years, many children forgot how to speak their languages or refused to. Jennie Blackbird spent six years at the Mohawk Institute School in Ontario before she returned home to visit. She told the TRC, "When I returned home I heard my Grandparents and family around me…speaking our language. I was a very angry person when I heard them speaking our Anishnaabe language. I remember telling my Grandparents 'don't you dare talk to me in that language' and feeling superior to them…now I regret having said that to my loved ones."

CHAPTER 4

A DAY AT SCHOOL

The residential school day started early and was carefully controlled throughout the day, allowing little or no private or social time for children to play. A bell woke up the children at 6:45 AM. This signaled them to wash and say prayers, then work at cleaning up their dormitory rooms until breakfast from 7:30 until 8:00 AM. During the morning, there would be religious classes run by either the Catholic Church or one of the Protestant missionary groups who ran the schools, then basic reading, writing, and arithmetic.

Life at the Blue Quills School in Alberta was a far cry from the life the children had lived with their families in the bush.

Classes were large—forty or fifty students was common—and there were often no textbooks, readers, or library books. Florence Bird remembered her school at Fort Chipewyan for the TRC: "School in my time was mostly memorizing. Not much teaching and talking. Lots of copying and memorizing. The sisters were not really teachers, but they did their best."

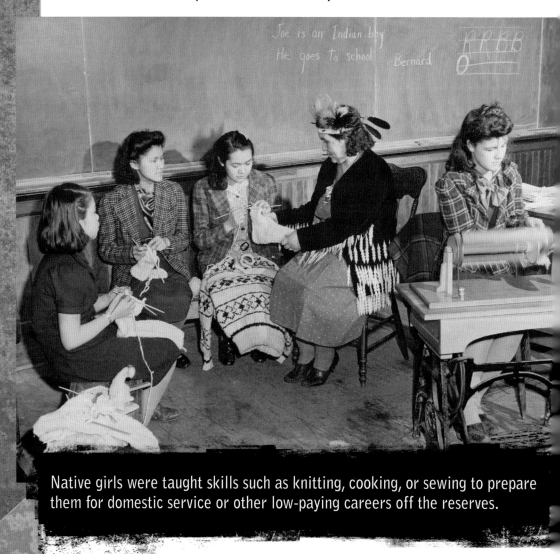

Native girls were taught skills such as knitting, cooking, or sewing to prepare them for domestic service or other low-paying careers off the reserves.

Most residential schools used a "half-day" system—education in the morning, work and training in the afternoon. After lunch, everybody was assembled to work. Younger students were sent to do garden work, laundry, or kitchen cleaning, while male senior students went to their jobs in the barn milking cows, working in the woodshop, or working in the blacksmith shop. Girls were taught to cook, sew, and train for domestic service as maids. Working in the school kitchen was very hard, as Rita Joe remembered for the TRC at Shubencadie in Nova Scotia: "For that you had to get up at four in the morning. We'd bake bread and we'd make porridge in a big, big pot and we'd boil over two hundred eggs…It was a lot of hard work that we did in the kitchen and the cook could be very cruel."

Many students felt they were not really being trained—they were simply being used for labor. Clayton Mack recalled to the TRC, "I helped look after the farm, helped with the potatoes, cut the hay. I tried to go to school but there was not enough time. I worked most of the time. I went to Alert Bay for school and instead they put me in a job!" The work training did not match the jobs many would find back at home. George Manuel at the Kamloops School remembered to the TRC, "Industrial training consisted of doing all the kinds of manual labor around the farm, except we did not have the kind of equipment that even an Indian of those days would have been using."

After work there might be time to play sports or socialize. Boys were kept separate from girls. After dinner there was a period for more prayers, and then lights out.

"WE WERE HUNGRY"

The food at the residential schools was cheap and often unhealthy, and there was rarely enough. Students were fed badly and often went hungry. Although farm products such as meat, dairy, and vegetables were produced at the schools as part of work training, most of these products were sold to produce income for the schools. If the Native students drank milk, it was skimmed first to take off the fat to make butter to sell. At the Aklavik School, Woodie Elias recalled to the TRC, "You didn't get enough: hungry! So once in a while we'd go raid the cellar and you can't call that stealing: that was our food."

At home students were raised on a diet of fresh "country food": freshly hunted meat and fish, fresh vegetables from the family garden, home-baked bannock bread. So students had a hard time with the strange food served at the residential schools. William Antoine told the TRC, "In the morning they gave you porridge, every morning…they called it 'mush' back then…it was lumpy, very lumpy…it didn't

Bannock, a simple biscuit dough baked beside a campfire, is based on an old Scottish recipe. It became a staple of Canadian Native and Métis families.

taste very good but you had to eat it in order to have some food in you…we got bread but no butter, just dry bread." At the Lestock School, John PeeAce told the TRC that he remembered walking past the teacher and staff dining room and seeing "they were having steak and chicken. It looked like a King's feast! And all we got were baloney sandwiches!" In 1944, the Indian Department inspected the Quappelle Valley Residential School, wrote Milloy, finding 28 percent of girls and 69 percent of boys were underweight.

Breaking the rules brought swift punishment. Teachers hit children with leather straps or with sticks. A child caught speaking his Native language could have his mouth washed out with soap. Some children were confined to isolated rooms and fed on bread and water for weeks or had their heads shaved for trying to escape. Rachel Chakasim went to the Fort Albany School in Ontario and recalled to the TRC, "I saw violence for the first time. I saw kids getting hit. Sometimes in the classroom a yardstick was used to hit. A nun would hit us…We never knew such fear before."

Children at the schools found themselves victims of abuse in many ways. Without trusted friends and relatives to protect them, some of the

Churches and missionary societies provided most of the staff at many residential schools. Very few of the teachers had any training in education.

students were sexually molested by members of the school staff or by other students. One boy told the TRC that one of the priests at the school told him, "God's going to punish you if you say anything. I fear God. I never said anything all these years." Another never reported her abuse because, "I thought I was the only one it was happening to. I thought it was just me." Native students were often told not to tell anybody about cases of abuse, and in most cases that were reported nothing was done. Sometimes the student was punished for reporting a case of abuse. Many chose to run away from school to escape their abusers. In some cases, older students would protect the younger ones, staying awake at night to keep abusers away while the younger children were asleep.

THE MUSH HOLE

One of the oldest residential schools was the Mohawk Institute, opened in 1829 and located on the Grand River Reserve in Brantford, Ontario. Run by the Anglican Church, the Mohawk Institute was originally set up to serve children from the Six Nations of the Iroquois, but after 1885 it began including First Nations students from other communities in Ontario. Known to the students as the "Mush Hole" (because of the poor food served there), it was one of the strictest schools: students received only three hours of education a day and the rest of the time was spent working on the school farm. Russ Moses told the *Ottawa Citizen*, "Our formal education was sadly neglected; when a child is tired, hungry, lice infested and treated as a sub-human, how in heaven's name do you expect to make a decent citizen out of him or her?" Children would wander into town for food. "It was our practice at the 'Mohawk' to go begging at various homes throughout Brantford. There were certain homes that we knew that the people were good to us, we would rap on the door and our question was: 'Anything extra,' whereupon if we were lucky, we would be rewarded with scraps from the household—survival of the fittest."

The Mohawk Institute was finally closed in 1970. The children who went there are all now elders who have become leaders in the effort to reveal the history of the residential school system. Today, an effort is being made to purchase the now rundown building as a memorial to the residential school experience.

A HOME FOR ILLNESS

Children arriving at the residential schools often fell ill. They had come from families that had lived outdoor lives with fresh food. Now they lived in overcrowded, confined buildings with poor sanitation and were served poor meals. Separated from their families, the children were lonely and often in shock, and in the close quarters of the dormitories diseases spread rapidly. To save money on heating, windows in the schools were often sealed shut. Without fresh air circulating diseases spread quickly. Tuberculosis, a lung disease that was often fatal if not treated, was the most common dangerous illness among children. At the Ermineskin School in Alberta, half the children had tuberculosis in 1930. Most schools did not have a doctor in residence and depended on visits from a regional Indian Department doctor or nurse. In 1907, the chief medical officer for Indian Affairs, Dr. Peter Bryce, published a shocking report on residential school health. The TRC reported that Bryce found that 24 percent of all aboriginal children who attended schools were dead by their graduation date. Many students discharged from schools died shortly after returning home, from 47 percent on the Piegan Reserve to 75 percent from File Hills Boarding School in Saskatchewan. In all, as many as six thousand children died while in the residential school system, according to the Truth and Reconciliation Committee. The chances of a child dying in a residential school were one in twenty-six, about the same (one in twenty-five) as a Canadian soldier dying in World War I.

CHAPTER 5

CLOSING THE SCHOOLS, HEALING THE WOUNDS

Canada's role in World War II brought a period of national confidence. Canada was no longer a frontier settlement. It had become a world leader. By the 1950s, Canada had settled its western prairies and was expanding its presence in the Arctic. The government had to admit that Canada's different Native cultures and identity had not simply disappeared. In a sense, the goal of assimilation had failed. Native children who had come out of the residential school system often found themselves caught between two worlds, without a real home in either one. John Tootoosis, a Cree First Nations leader told the TRC that, "when an Indian comes out of these places it is like being put between two walls in a room and left hanging in the middle. On one side there are all the things he learned from his people and their way of life is being wiped out. On the other side there are the whiteman's ways which he could never fully understand since he never had the right amount of education and could not be a part of it."

"THE HAPPIEST THING WE EVER HEARD"

In 1951, the Canadian House of Commons and Senate revised the Indian Act. Native religious ceremonies were no longer banned. The new act stated that, "whenever and wherever

Graduates of the residential schools found themselves torn between two cultures. It was difficult to return to the old ways and just as hard to adapt to new ones.

possible Indian children should be educated with other children." The residential schools had become expensive failures. During World War II, the Canadian government faced a shortage of money for education and decided that sending students to local day schools would be cheaper than building new residential schools. Instead of trying to destroy Native identity, the day schools would try to bring Native children into the Canadian school system. The role of church missionaries was weakened as schools began to hire more qualified teaching staff. The process of closing the schools continued over forty years. The last closed in 1986. When a teacher announced that the Shubencadie School in Nova Scotia was closing forever in 1967, student Rose Marie Prosper remembered it for the TRC: "It was the happiest thing we ever heard…we all jumped out of our chairs, we banged our desks, our books went flying, we hugged each other…We were crying, and we were laughing. It was the best, best thing we ever heard."

In some cases, Native communities feared that closing the residential schools would deprive them of any education for their children. In 1970, the Cree community of Blue Quills First Nation, Alberta, protested against church control of the local residential school and peacefully occupied the building, demanding that it be turned over to the local band. Blue Quills became the first college that was Native owned and operated in Canada. Today, it offers advanced college degrees, training, and even courses in the Cree language.

NATIVE SCHOOLS, NATIVE GOALS

First Nations schools are now focusing on education that looks to the future for Native children. Skills that are needed for modern jobs are carefully taught, and the problems that plague children on reserves are carefully addressed. Native children in Canada are four times more likely to commit suicide than non-Native children. Alcohol and drugs remain a major problem in rural communities that have struggled with the loss of Native culture. Many Native schools are working to bridge the cultural gap left by the residential school system. The Shingwauk School in Ontario was one of the original Native residential schools.

Canadian children today are encouraged to learn about and respect First Nations heritage. Schools actively promote cross-cultural understanding.

Today, the Shingwauk Kinoomaage Gamig ("Teaching Lodge") in Ontario is working with Algoma University to offer courses in Anishnaabe culture and languages in a partnership that respects the cultures of both schools.

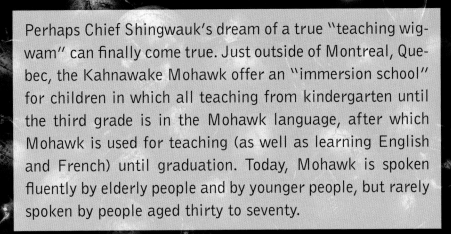

Perhaps Chief Shingwauk's dream of a true "teaching wig-wam" can finally come true. Just outside of Montreal, Quebec, the Kahnawake Mohawk offer an "immersion school" for children in which all teaching from kindergarten until the third grade is in the Mohawk language, after which Mohawk is used for teaching (as well as learning English and French) until graduation. Today, Mohawk is spoken fluently by elderly people and by younger people, but rarely spoken by people aged thirty to seventy.

While the residential schools were gradually closing, aboriginal children still faced being removed from their families. The 1951 Indian Act allowed individual provinces to take responsibility for children. Many social welfare agencies believed that aboriginal children would have a better education in the public school system if they were taken from their families and adopted or placed with foster homes in towns and cities. Thousands of children were "scooped up" in what became known as "the sixties scoop."

In 1963, the Canadian government prepared an official report on Canada's Native peoples. The H.B. Hawthorne report found, "The schooling of Indian children today raises many questions. School for some of them is unpleasant, frightening and painful. For these and for some others it is not so much adaptive as maladaptive. They have little reason to like or to be interested in the school in any way." The study claimed that Native people were Canada's "citizens minus" (meaning they were minus certain rights) and that they now needed to be treated as "citizens plus." The report urged the government to work with local First Nations bands to solve the problem of improving education for Native children. It was also harshly critical of the way the Department of Indian Affairs worked.

THE WHITE PAPER

In 1969, Prime Minister Pierre Trudeau and his minister for Indian Affairs, Jean Chretien, presented a "White Paper" that proposed abolishing the Indian Act entirely and ending the special legal relationship between First Nations and the Canadian government. Natives would be treated simply as any other Canadian citizen, without regard to historical treaties or rights.

Prime Minister Pierre Trudeau represented a new, younger image for Canada. He thought that the Indian Act was out of date and should be scrapped.

Aboriginal communities felt that the White Paper proposals would put them at a disadvantage and take away the legal rights guaranteed to the First Nations. In 1970, Harold Cardinal, a young leader in the Cree community of Alberta, published an answer, called "The Red Paper," which later became a bestselling book, *The Unjust Society*. Cardinal wrote that the solutions offered by the government's White Paper were "a program which offers nothing better than cultural genocide... extermination through assimilation" and called on Canada to respect Native rights, writing, "I find that as Indian people we share hopes for a better Canada, a better future and a better deal. We share hopes that Canadian society will accept us as we are and listen to what we have to say."

Acceptance of Native people's rights did not always come easily, especially when land and resources were in question. When local bands and Native communities began to assert their rights, conflicts did arise. When a local golf course threatened Mohawk First Nation land at Oka, near Montreal, protests spilled into an armed standoff in 1990 between the Canadian armed forces and the Mohawk Warrior society. Again, in 1995 when the Shuswap people attempted to reclaim land they held sacred, they were confronted with Royal Canadian Mounted Police at Gustafsen Lake, British Columbia. In 2012, a bill was presented to the Canadian House of Commons that would have rewritten the Indian Act and opened aboriginal land to industrial use. Led by four women—three Natives and one non-Native—Native Canadians organized protests and teach-ins to be "Idle No More"—a call that is still an active struggle in Canada today.

The road to reconciliation is not easy. Native communities continue to struggle, and many problems still need to be addressed.

HEALING THE WOUNDS

The last residential school closed in 1996, but the social and mental trauma endured by generations of Native children take a long time to heal. In 2006, the Canadian Federal Courts approved the Indian Residential Schools Settlement Agreement, which agreed to pay more than $2 billion Canadian in damages to eighty thousand survivors of the residential school system. On June 11, 2008, Canadian prime minister Stephen Harper gave a speech apologizing on behalf of the government of Canada, recorded by the Indigenous and Northern Affairs Canada: "Today, we recognize that this policy of assimilation was wrong, has caused great harm, and has no place in our country...The government now recognizes that the consequences of the Indian Residential Schools policy were profoundly negative and that this policy has had a lasting and damaging impact on Aboriginal culture, heritage and language."

In 2008, the Truth and Reconciliation Commission of Canada was formed. It gathers and publishes the stories of survivors of the residential school system.

Native people want to maintain their identity and culture. They have struggled for hundreds of years to continue living on the land that gave them life and identity. The Canadian prime minister's apology from the Indigenous and Northern Affairs Canada builds a road to travel for the future:

There is no place in Canada for the attitudes that inspired the Indian Residential Schools system to ever prevail again...The Government of Canada sincerely apologizes and asks the forgiveness of the Aboriginal peoples of this country for failing them so profoundly.

Nous le regrettons

We are sorry

Nimitataynan

Niminchinowesamin

Mamiattugut

1534 Jacques Cartier discovers the Saint Lawrence River and claims the land in the name of the king of France.

1763 France cedes, or surrenders, its lands in North America to Great Britain at the end of the Seven Years' War, also known as the French and Indian War.

1831 The Mohawk School opens in Brantford, Ontario, making it the oldest residential school in Canada. It originally serves the Loyalist Iroquois First Nations and finally closes in 1970.

1832 Anishnaabe chief Shingwauk travels by snowshoe from the Great Lakes to Toronto to ask the governor for help in building a school for Native children.

1857 The Gradual Civilization Act is passed. It requires any Indian who speaks English or French and has education to become enfranchised as a citizen and lose Indian rights.

1867 The passing of the Constitution Act creates the Dominion of Canada. It consists of the colony of Canada, which split into French-speaking Quebec and English-speaking Ontario, Nova Scotia, and New Brunswick.

1876 The Indian Act is passed, which gives the government the right to create laws regarding Indians and Indian lands. This act identifies who is an Indian and establishes Native legal rights.

1879 The Davin Report is published, calling for the creation of residential "industrial" schools to separate children from their homes and promote assimilation.

1885 Facing starvation, Louis Riel leads Métis and Cree followers in the North West Rebellion. The uprising is put down, and Riel and eight Cree are hanged for treason. The Trans-Canada railway is completed.

1900 Seventy residential schools are operating across Canada.

1920 Deputy superintendent of Indian Affairs Duncan Campbell Scott makes residential school attendance mandatory for Indian children between the ages of seven and fifteen.

1958 Indian Affairs regional inspectors recommend abolition of residential schools. Sixty schools remain open in 1960, when Indians are finally allowed to vote.

1969 The Trudeau government proposes a White Paper to redefine Native rights, which is quickly opposed by First Nations leaders, such as Harold Cardinal.

1982 The Canadian Constitution Act is amended and now recognizes the rights of "Indian, Inuit, and Métis peoples of Canada."

1990 The Oka Crisis, between the Mohawk Nation and the town of Oka, Quebec, lasts six months. It is the first in a series of violent conflicts between aboriginal peoples and the Canadian government.

1996 The last Indian residential school, Gordon Indian Residential School in Saskatchewan, closes.

2006 The federal government, legal representatives of former students, the Assembly of First Nations, Inuit representatives, and churches sign the Indian Residential School Settlement Agreement.

2008 Prime Minister Stephen Harper apologizes on behalf of Canada to survivors of the residential school system.

2015 The Truth and Reconciliation Commission of Canada, formed in 2008 to examine the history and trauma of the residential school system, delivers its final report in June.

GLOSSARY

aboriginal Relating to the descendants of the original inhabitants of North America. The Canadian Constitution recognizes three groups of aboriginal people: Indians, Métis, and Inuit.

amendment A change or addition to a law.

Anishnaabe The name for the Algonquian people also known as Ojibwe, Chippewa, Odawa, and Mississauga.

annihilate To totally wipe out or eliminate; to defeat completely.

assimilation The process of becoming a part, or making someone become a part, of a group, country, or a society.

band In Canada, an Indian band, sometimes called a First Nations band or simply a First Nation, is the basic unit of government for peoples covered by the Indian Act.

bannock A simple kind of biscuit bread baked on a campfire.

Cree A First Nation with communities reaching from Labrador to British Columbia, speaking variations of the Algonquian nêhiyaw language.

dominion A country that was part of the British Empire but had its own government.

dormitory Building on a school campus that has rooms where students can live.

enfranchisement Giving someone the legal right to vote in elections.

First Nation A term that came into common usage in the 1970s to replace the word "Indian," which some people found offensive. Although the term "First Nation" is widely used, no legal definition of it exists. Some Indian peoples have also adopted the term "First Nation" to replace the word "band" in the name of their community.

genocide The deliberate killing of people who belong to a particular racial, political, or cultural group.

House of Commons The lower house of the British and Canadian parliaments.

Inuit An aboriginal people in northern Canada, who in the past (and in the United States) were called "Eskimo." The word means "people" in the Inuit language.

Métis People of mixed First Nation and European ancestry who identify themselves as Métis, as distinct from First Nations people, Inuit, or non-aboriginal people.

missionary A person who is sent to a foreign country to do religious work (such as to convince people to join a religion or to help people who are sick or poor).

pemmican A dried food made from buffalo meat and fat, often pounded together with berries.

Potlatch A lavish ceremonial meal and celebration by North American Native Americans.

reserve An area of land, the legal title to which is held by the crown, set apart for the use and benefit of an Indian band.

status Indian A person who is registered as an Indian under the Canadian Indian Act.

superintendent A person who directs or manages a department or acts as manager for an Indian reserve.

treaty An official agreement that is made between two or more countries or groups.

voyageur A French-Canadian word used for the trappers and fur traders who traveled and traded by canoe.

Amnesty International Canada
312 Laurier Ave E
Ottawa, ON K1N 1H9
Canada
(613) 744-7667
Website: http://www.amnesty.ca
Amnesty International works globally to represent human rights, including those of indigenous communities in Canada and internationally.

The Assembly of First Nations (AFN)
55 Metcalfe Street, Suite 1600
Ottawa, ON K1P 6L5
Canada
(866) 869-6789
Website: http://www.afn.ca
The Assembly of First Nations (AFN) is a Native representative organization of First Nations represented by their chiefs.

Inuit Tapiriit Kanatami
75 Albert Street, Suite 1101
Ottawa, ON K1P 5E7
Canada

(866) 262-8181

Website: http://www.itk.ca

Inuit Tapiriit Kanatami (ITK) is the national voice of fifty-five thousand Inuit living in fifty-three communities across the Inuvialuit Settlement Region (Northwest Territories), Nunavut, Nunavik (northern Quebec), and Nunatsiavut (northern Labrador) land claims regions. Inuit call this vast region Inuit Nunangat.

Legacy of Hope Foundation

75 Albert Street, Suite 301

Ottawa ON K1P 5E7

Canada

(613) 237-4806

Website: http://www.legacyofhope.ca

The Legacy of Hope Foundation prepares educational materials for understanding the history of Native residential schools and reconciliation efforts, with a website featuring downloadable books and information.

The Truth and Reconciliation Commission of Canada

1500-360 Main Street

Winnipeg, MB R3C 3Z3

Canada

(888) 872-5554 (888-TRC-5554)

Email: info@trc.ca

Website: http://www.trc.ca

The Truth and Reconciliation Commission is tasked to learn the truth about what happened in the residential schools and to inform all Canadians about what happened there. The commission hopes to guide and inspire First Nations, Inuit, and Métis peoples and Canadians in a process of truth and healing. Downloadable reports and extensive information are available.

WEBSITES

Because of the changing nature of Internet links, Rosen Publishing has developed an online list of websites related to the subject of this book. This site is updated regularly. Please use this link to access the list:

http://www.rosenlinks.com/BWGE/canada

André, Julie-Ann. *We Feel Good Out Here = Zhik gwaa'an, nakhwatthaiitat qwiinzii* (The Land Is Our Storybook). Calgary, AB: Fifth House, 2008.

Ellis, Deborah. *Looks Like Daylight: Voices of Indigenous Kids.* Toronto, ON: Groundwood Books, 2013.

Fontaine, Theodore. *Broken Circle: The Dark Legacy of Indian Residential Schools.* Victoria, BC: Heritage House Publishing, 2010.

Friedman, Mark D. *Genocide* (Hot Topics). Chicago, IL: Heinemann Library, 2012.

Gordon, Irene Ternier. *People on the Move: The Métis of the Western Plains.* Victoria, BC: Heritage House Publishing 2011.

Hill, Gord. *500 Years of Resistance Comic Book.* Toronto, ON: University of Toronto Press, 2010.

January, Brendan. *Genocide: Modern Crimes Against Humanity.* Brookfield CT: Twenty-First Century Books, 2014. Ebook.

Jordan-Fenton, Christie. *A Stranger at Home: A True Story.* Toronto, ON: Annick Press, 2011.

Robinson, David Alexander. *7 Generations: The Pact: A Plains Cree Saga.* Winnipeg, MB: Portage and Main Press, 2012.

Sellers, Bev. *They Called Me Number One: Secrets and Survival at an Indian Residential School.* Vancouver, BC: Talon Books, 2013.

Silvie, Ihek'atem Diane. *The Kids Book of Aboriginal Peoples in Canada.* Toronto, ON: Kids Can Press, 2012.

Cardinal, Harold. *The Unjust Society*. Seattle, WA: University of Washington Press, 1999. Retrieved December 22, 2015 (http://www.sfu.ca/~palys/Cardinal-1969-ExcerptFromTheUnjust-Society.pdf).

Daschuk, James. *Clearing the Plains: Disease, Politics of Starvation, and the Loss of Aboriginal Life*. Regina, SK: University of Regina Press, 2013.

General Synod of the Anglican Church of Canada. "The Mohawk Institute—Brantford, Ontario." The Anglican Church of Canada, 2015. Retrieved December 1, 2015 (http://www.anglican.ca/tr/histories/mohawk-institute).

Hawthorne, H. B, ed. Canadian Indian Affairs Report: *A Survey of the Contemporary Indians of Canada—Economic, Political, Educational Needs and Policies*, 1967. Retrieved December 22, 2015 (https://www.aadnc-aandc.gc.ca/DAM/DAM-INTER-HQ/STAGING/texte-text/ai-arp-ls-pubs-sci3_1326997109567_eng.pdf).

Henderson, Jennifer. *Reconciling Canada: Critical Perspectives on the Culture of Redress* Toronto, ON: University of Toronto Press, 2013.

Indigenous and Northern Affairs Canada. "Statement of Apology to Former Students of Indian Residential Schools." Government of Canada, September 15, 2009. Retrieved December 1, 2015 (https://www.aadnc-aandc.gc.ca/eng/110010001 5644/1100100015649).

Johnstone, Basil. *Indian School Days*. Norman, OK: University of Oklahoma Press, 1988.

Loyie, Larry. *Residential Schools with the Words and Images of Survivors*. Brantford, ON: Indigenous Education Press, 2014.

McGregor, Heather. *Inuit Education and Schools in the Eastern Arctic*. Vancouver, BC: University of British Columbia Press, 2010.

McKegney, Sam. *Magic Weapons: Aboriginal Writers Remaking Community After Residential School*. Winnipeg, MB: University of Manitoba Press, 2007.

Miller, J. R. *Shingwauk's Vision: A History of Native Residential Schools*. Toronto, ON: University of Toronto Press, 1996.

Milloy, John. *A National Crime: The Canadian Government and the Residential School System 1879–1986*. Winnipeg, MB: University of Manitoba Press, 2006.

Moses, Russ. "'The Most Abject Human Misery': Memories of a Residential School Survivor." *Ottawa Citizen,* May 18, 2015. Retrieved December 1, 2015 (http://ottawacitizen.com/news/national/the-most-abject-human-misery-memories-of-a-residential-school-survivor).

Niezen, Ronald. *Truth and Indignation: Canada's Truth and Reconciliation Commission on Indian Residential Schools*. Toronto, ON: University of Toronto Press, 2103.

Nishnawbe Aski Nation. "Residential School Survivor Stories." 2015. Retrieved December 1, 2015 (http://rschools.nan.on.ca/article/survivor-stories-4.asp).

Regan, Paulette. *Unsettling the Settler Within: Indian Residential*

Schools, Truth Telling, and Reconciliation in Canada. Vancouver, BC: University of British Columbia Press 2011.

Smithsonian Institution. "Kill the Indian and Save the Man." Smithsonian National Museum of Natural History. Retrieved December 22, 2015 (http://americanhistory.si.edu/do-++++cumentsgallery/exhibitions/ledger_drawing_3.htm).

Timpson, Annis May, ed. *First Nations, First Thoughts: The Impact of Indigenous Thought in Canada.* Vancouver, BC: University of British Columbia Press, 2009.

Truth and Reconciliation Commission of Canada. *Final Report of the Truth and Reconciliation Commission of Canada.* Toronto, ON: Lorimer and Company Publishers. Retrieved December 1, 2015 (http://www.myrobust.com/websites/trcinstitution/File/Interim%20report%20English%20electronic.pdf).

Truth and Reconciliation Commission of Canada. *The Survivors Speak: A Report.* Winnipeg, MB, May 30, 2015. Retrieved December 1, 2015 (http://www.trc.ca/websites/trcinstitution/File/2015/Findings/Survivors_Speak_2015_05_30_web_o.pdf).

Truth and Reconciliation Commission of Canada. *They Came for the Children: Canada, Aboriginal Children, and Residential Schools.* Winnipeg, MB, 2015. Retrieved December 1, 2015 (http://www.myrobust.com/websites/trcinstitution/File/2039_T&R_eng_web%5B1%5D.pdf).

United Nations Convention on the Prevention and Punishment of the Crime of Genocide. United Nations, 1948. Retrieved December 22, 2015 (https://treaties.un.org/doc/Publication/UNTS/Volume%2078/volume-78-I-1021-English.pdf).

Woolford, Andrew, ed. *Colonial Genocide in Indigenous North America*. Durham, NC: Duke University Press, 2014.

INDEX

ABOUT THE AUTHOR

Robert Z. Cohen was born in New York City and studied anthropology at Boston University, concentrating on African and Native American languages and mythology. He traveled around the Caribbean researching memories of African languages. Cohen moved to Europe to research the language and music of the Romani (Gypsy) people in Macedonia, Romania, and Hungary, as well as searching out the last echoes of Yiddish music in Europe. He was a founder and editor of the newspaper *Budapest Week* and a writer for publications such as *Time Out Budapest.* He lives in Budapest, Hungary, and works as a journalist and travel guide writer. He leads his own Klezmer band on tours around Europe and North America.

PHOTO CREDITS